Inuring Lassitude

Abigail Esther Nair

BookLeaf Publishing
India | USA | UK

Presentation by *BookLeaf Publishing*

Web: www.bookleafpub.com

E-mail: info@bookleafpub.com

ISBN: 9789358739060

First edition 2021

1 Glass eyes shattering as the tears of endearment

that once stroked my pitiful ego fall from my

barren face.

The cracks on the surface begin to travel and split,

my body conceding as the pain runs laps around

my being.

Glass skin releasing gold matter gushed through

the crevices of my hull;

Fall to the floor droplets of folklore,

Become red before Solomon's door and plea for

wisdom in order to attain salvation.

The creation of Adam,

The fall am I,

God said see to it that Lucifer will never fly-

Let his wings be plucked and may he roam the
Earth for seducing Eve with a worthless pile of
dirt.

Demons and Angels,

The puppet was I;

I wish you could hear the sound of my flesh as it
cried.

Shards scattered on the mezzanine,

My frail body can no longer contain this sin…

Full to the brim,

I'm on the floor,

The evil in my mind will not rescind.

The glass has cracked will God still let me in?

2 I wish I could live the life I painted within my words…

3 Individual

Individualism is a curse I cast upon myself
unknowingly;

Now isolation is my only friend.

4 For You My Love

If moonlight were kisses,

I'd bathe you in it's incandescent glow...

· I'd kiss the torn parts of your lilac skin as your eyes
wept raging waterfulls.

If my voice were honey,

I'd immerse you in it's sweet intensity...

Coating seething wounds designed by unkindness;

letting my mouth aperture to create a necklace
made of nectar to sit ever so delicately on your
chest-

all so that you may know the taste of sweet words
as they glazed over your being.

If my touch was of an angels wings,

I'd pluck my flesh so that you may experience the gaiety of the seventh heaven.

For you my love,

I'd sell my soul to the birds above,

I'd open my heart and let God delve into my cavity's to excavate my sources of alimentation;

But alas-

I am simply a man who wishes to be your beloved dijin.

So for you my love...

I will scour the universe with my meagre mortality

just to see your eyes light up the earth once more.

5 The Evil Eye

The white man warns of the evil eye,

He says

"Beware! for it bewitches, this is the type of voodoo

that belongs solely to witches."

Incense and prayer, readings and gemstones;

Are taken far from home to a place unknown.

Stripped of their nature,

their origin and dwelling,

Our crafts are taken for the white mans peddling.

He tells venomous tales to our people which make

us die scared,

Whilst believing in a religion that was forced onto

us,

not shared.

He then turns around to his white mass and says

"Hush its okay for they don't know that I've taken
their tools of wisdom to be only for us."

"These white men are dangerous" my grandfather
warns;

and now that I've grown up I can see their white
privilege coming for me with numerous thorns.

Ancestors and guardians weeping from above,

For the blood shed and exploitation they continue
to witness is all too much.

Lost and stolen generations which were ahead of
their time,

in both knowledge and power of the human mind;

I can hear my predecessors mourn in sync as they

begin their final cries my heart starts to sink.

The history and the power of the soul is now

buried within the white mans time,

far away from my peoples reach-

When suddenly a white woman unearths our

treasures and decides to speak...

Speaking on topics where she has not been

sanctioned to utter,

She will steal and take another's culture all in the

name of charter.

"These white women are dangerous" my

grandmother warns;

and now that I've grown up I can see their white
privilege coming for me with more than just
thorns.

The cycle continues and as I grow tired,

I remember the white folk who declared through a
guise that they were simply 'inspired'.

So,

awake I lay thinking of The Evil Eye and the white
woman with the power;

to just...cry.

6 Out Of Mind!

An enigmatic blackhole was she.

Bones screaming in agony and echoing through the crevices of her soul.

Blood scraping the walls of her consciousness pleading for stability or release;

Jumping through halos bestowed from the light above...

While watching black doves fly-

We shall stare as the little girl cries.

Mind breaking,

Body aching-

She traverses the universes worlds of lonliness,

Dimensions of suffering inconceivable to man,

Dancing with shackles of crippling despair;

Finding euphoria through means of physical
ailment.

Spewing snakes bearing flowers with a deceptive
charm...

She is seducing Gods into the whirlwind which is
twisting within her solar system;

This keeps her stars aligned and meteors raging.

The blackhole approaches.

Soul sucking,

Mind turning,

Third eye opening,

Oh what it means to be alive in the silence of her ravenous yet beguiling mind!

7 Haven

There was once a place I would call a haven.

I'm not sure what it looked or felt like;

Maybe it was a dream that I waded too far into,

Encountering blissful memories of life that was
never mine...

Gave me a strange peace as a child,

it helped me survive.

I want to revisit my coven of all things pure,

Things that a child would find joy in;

Simple things like,

the taste of candy,

The smell of food,

And-

The sight of family…

8 Thief

I am unsure of where it began…

Who set the button of realisation off in my mind?

Who dared to defy the palace of chaos which
resides in my souls sacredly sanctimonious
sanctuary;

All to make me aware of what I was doing...

What was I doing?

I was looking for happiness,

My purpose,

My validation,

My reason for existing.

The reason for my tiresome and lifeless
breathing…

I was looking for my colour within other
exhibitions of art devoid of life;

The people around me.

I begged and pleaded for creations to give me an
answer,

I begged beings who I thought were creators,

'Gods' amongst men-

When in reality they were nothing more than I
was.

I was distracting myself…

Who told me?

Who?

Why did you have to tell me…

Why couldn't you have let me blindly chase and inflate the egos of petty beings as I belittled myself with laughter from other's and took memories that weren't mine to fuel my will to live.

It was going so well-

Who are you to tell me that I'm using everyone else's moments to distract myself from my own empty ones.

I see it.

When I run out of abstractions I hear the resentful
silence that is my life.

It turns out you can only steal other people's
moments for so long-

before they become less appealing and appetising
to your ravenous soul.

It isn't fair,

I don't know where to go-

It's empty how do I make my moments again?

I can't.

I can't.

I can't.

Im frozen,

I'm stuck in a cold room with no walls and a damp floor that is my mind.

WHO ARE YOU TO MAKE ME REALISE THAT IM STEALING JOY BECAUSE I CANT ESCAPE MY OWN SORROWS?!

Oh...

that's right,

You're me.

A thief's home is always empty in the sense that nothing truly belongs to him.

9 I Love Myself?

I'll love myself through the eyes of someone else–

An unconditional and pure love that I'll never see myself with.

10 The Dark and I

My soles glide across the black marble pond,

making ripples as I go;

I begin to balance on the balls of my feet as the soft
fabric that is draped upon my skin comes to a halt
from my expedition across the sea.

Goosebumps litter my bare skin as the icy breeze
gives me a warm embrace-

In a room dimly lit by the suns gloomy glare.

I continue to dance across the ocean floor,

Black skin,

Black dress,

Black Sea of marble.

Cracks of marble gaze upon me as I laugh,

The piano begins to creak out a sweet melody
through the crevices of its smile as my euphoric
and satiate laughter echoes throughout the vacuous
space.

I'll dance happily on my own in the void,

Till someone dares to join me in the beautiful yet
wild depths of the dark and I's mysterious dance of
chaotic jubilance...

11 3:30 AM

26

Astonishingly antagonising was the realisation and materialisation of my existence.

Let me decimate my remaining prerequisites for the sake of the inequities which I instilled soon myself;

So that my soul my live in bliss unharmed by the biased judgment which is placed upon my being.

Permeate my organs with desire for limerence so that I may obtain the atrocious normality which this society claims to rescind.

I lay supine while an abhorrent irrationality and a beguiling sense of madness pollute my headspace.

I question the very reality which was fabricated in
order for the manifestation of my fallacies to
coexist with the beliefs from the unknown
universe.

Streaming into my mind of existential depression
the stars spin and the world collapses,

Waterfalls pool into blackholes,

Earthquakes dismantle the stars,

Planets made from oceans quiver,

Clouds of grass float lazily around;

As I continue to lay supine and ponder the reason
for my momentary existence-

The crickets chirp in the deafening silence of the
night,

Far beyond my mind's ethereal and delectable
delusion...

It is now 3:30 AM.

12 Doubt

Taking root in the crevices of my mind,

A small trickle of doubt begins to pollute my
thinking.

The droplets turned into rivers of fire as they
caressed the dips and shape which is engraved into
my brain;

I winch in pain as my eyes cry red,

And my vision becomes blurred.

Everything I touched was now being painted with
a pollen called doubt,

Creating black flowers of greed which swallowed
my happiness with questions of 'what if..'
And hissings of,

'It isn't true-'

'He doesn't love you'...

Black flowers,

Red tears,

And a blurred vision made me see you as
something you weren't…

Heartless.

I'll try to clear my perception from the dye that's
polluting my line of sight-

I hope you'll stay to whisper words of reassurance
and care while I close my eyes to clear my vision;

But this is reality...

And now that I've reopened the windows of my

soul to gaze upon what hope lies before me,

All I see is–

Fields of black flowers,

Red tears of fire,

Blurred sight,

And a bleeding heart;

With doubt smiling at me from the deepest part.

13 let's dance

I took off my shoes and tasted the water that fell
upon my face,

Trickling down the crevices of my body and
causing my skin to rust.

Your animus glare cut my delicate flesh as I danced
in the rain,

I felt depraved,

Nourished,

But oddly sane...

I'll follow the cascading tears with my eyes as my
joints attempt to egress from each-other;

Erosion polluting my membrane as each drop falls
from the grey abyss above.

You gazed upon my corroding figure with a fiery intensity;

And in that moment I came to the realisation that my degradation was your secret symphony.

"Let's dance"

-said you, the puppeteer.

14 The Shower

The ukulele plays an eloquent sound,

While the smell of petrichor seeps in through the vents.

The melody resounding from a single device,

Instilled me with a sorrowful debt.

Scalding my skin,

Crafting an Icy sonorous wind,

The water is falling all around.

Steam sticking to the windows,

Permeating my lungs,

The nefarious silence dared to make sound.

The ethereal glow radiating from the window outside,

makes me question what it's really like to be alive...

I lye supine,

String up into the glum iridescence sculpted by the mist and luminous hues.

The water continues to scald my broken skin as my desire for limerence becomes desolate.

The liquid pools into my stomach as I breathe in-

Pollutes my eyes upon opening;

And reminds me what its like to be living a life filled with sin.

15 When We Are Older

When we are older,

I hope to travel serene landscapes with you,

To pass by seas of sapphire and marvel sand.

When we are older,

I hope to hear your voice radiate from the front
seat as I'm sprawled across the back gazing out the
window with child like bewilderment.

When we are older,

I hope to sway you into halting our journey so that
we may walk among the road devoid of life,

So that we may look upon the trees and grasslands
of decay,

Brown and tired but ever so vibrant;

A copy of us.

When we are older,

I hope to see your face reflecting off of the mirror
as you speak to me with your melancholic hues.

Such a somber tune is emitted from your voice,

But despite your aura I feel at peace knowing your
there,

Even if you no longer view me with the same
limerence as before.

You vacated my life long ago but your scent still
lingers in my dreams,

It both haunts and entices me to fall into a falsified
intimacy with you,

Not the kind that makes your body quiver,

But the kind that makes you feel whole from the bottom of your soul.

But your ethereal being is no longer in my life.

So if we get older…

I hope to traverse the universes ever expanding arms with you by my side,

I hope to breathe in the air that kisses the sea goodnight and greets the sun good morning at first light,

I hope to see a wide array of colours pass by the apertures of our souls with immense zest and alacrity.

And lastly...

I hope to see you;

Smiling at me,

From the front seat.

16 Dreams

Dreams are the broken Neverland we can never return to.

Dreams are the doorstep into the realm of wonder where we ponder our existence through the enlightenment of vanity.

Dreams help us paint a false reality which we will never inhabit,

They help us escape our world of colourless colours.

…When I dream,

Worlds of new and old collide to make a masterpiece in which I can live out my falsified happiness.

My dreams create what my body cannot regulate
on its own,

The fibre of what it means to feel in purest form.

My dreams enable my existential questions to
answer them selves-

Or form new ones;

Above all,

My dreams create mellifluous hymns of song and
yellow clouds made of whiskey and gin sing along,

I'll sink my melancholic into this fountain of youth,

As my dreams give me the life I desire to pursuer
but could never achieve in my epoch.

My dreams create a wide array of colours in the
most abstract form,

Trees of red,

Grasslands of blue,

Seas of green,

Most of these things remain unseen,

But not in my dreams.

In my dreams the seen becomes unseen and the unseen becomes seen.

I can fly with wings of candy and breathe in air permeated with gold.

The sun is cold,

The moon is hot,

My dreams are everything I'm not.